D1320079

Also by Paul Muldoon

New Weather (1973)
Mules (1977)
Why Brownlee Left (1980)
Quoof (1983)
Meeting the British (1987)
Selected Poems 1968–1986 (1987)

The Faber Book of Contemporary Irish Poetry
(editor) (1986)

MADOC

A Mystery

MADOC
A Mystery

Paul Muldoon

Farrar Straus Giroux

New York

Copyright © 1991 by Paul Muldoon
All rights reserved
First published in 1990 by Faber and Faber Ltd., London
Printed in the United States of America
First American edition, 1991

Library of Congress Cataloging-in-Publication Data
Muldoon, Paul.
Madoc : a mystery / Paul Muldoon.— 1st American ed.
"First published in the United Kingdom in 1991 by Faber and Faber
Ltd"—T.p. verso.
I. Title.
PR6063.U367M34   1991   823'.914—dc20   90-27876   CIP

Grateful acknowledgements are due to the editors of Antaeus,
the London Review of Books, the New Statesman, the Observer,
The State of the Language, the Sunday Times, 32 Counties and
The Times Literary Supplement; also to the Corporation of Yaddo
and the MacDowell Colony, for their generous hospitality.

ISBN 13: 978-0-374-52344-2

for Jean

Contents

PART ONE

The Key, 3

Tea, 5

Capercaillies, 6

Asra, 8

The Panther, 9

Cauliflowers, 10

The Briefcase, 12

PART TWO

MADOC—*A Mystery*, 13

Part One

Part One

The Key

I ran into Foley six months ago in a dubbing suite in
Los Angeles. He was half-way through post-
production on a remake of *The Hoodlum Priest*, a film
for which I've a special affection since my cousin,
Marina McCall, was an extra in the first version. She
had worked as a nanny for various movie stars,
including Tippi Hedren, and seemed to spend half her
time in the sky between New York and LA. Though I
sat through three or four showings of *The Hoodlum
Priest* in the Olympic Cinema, Moy, and carefully
scrutinized the crowd scenes, I was never able to point
to Marina with anything like conviction.

Foley was working on a sequence involving a police
line-up, in which the victim shuffled along, stopped
with each suspect in turn, then shuffled on. At a
critical moment, she dropped a key on the floor. Foley
was having trouble matching sound to picture on this
last effect. I was struck by the fact that, just as early
radio announcers had worn dinner-jackets, he was
wearing an ultramarine tuxedo. After half a dozen
attempts, he decided to call it quits, and emerged from
his sound booth like a diver from a bathyscope. He
offered me a tidbit that tasted only of mesquite.

I wanted to say something about Marina, something
about an 'identity parade' in which I once took part,
something about the etymology of 'tuxedo', but I
found myself savouring the play between 'booth' and
'bathy-', 'quits' and 'mesquite', and began to
'misquote' myself:

When he sookied a calf down a boreen
it was through Indo-European.
When he clicked at a donkey carting dung
your grandfather had an African tongue.
You seem content to ventriloquize the surf.

Foley swallowed whatever it was:

Still defending that same old patch of turf?
Have you forgotten that 'hoodlum' is back-slang
for the leader of a San Francisco street-gang?

He flounced off into his cubicle. Though this, our only
exchange, was remarkable for its banality, Foley has
had some profound effect on me. These past six
months I've sometimes run a little ahead of myself, but
mostly I lag behind, my footfalls already pre-empted
by their echoes.

Tea

I was rooting through tea-chest after tea-chest
as they drifted in along Key West

when I chanced on 'Pythagoras in America':
the book had fallen open at a book-mark

of tea; a tassel
of black watered silk from a Missal;

a tea-bird's black tail-feather.
All I have in the house is some left-over

squid cooked in its own ink
and this unfortunate cup of tea. Take it. Drink.

Capercaillies

In a deep, in a dark wood, somewhere north of Loch
    Lomond,
Saint Joan and I should be in our element;
the electroplated bracken and furze
have only gradually given way to pines and firs

in which a – what? – a straggler from Hadrian's
sixth legion squats over the latrine
and casts a die. His spurs suggest a renegade
Norman knight, as does his newly-prinked

escutcheon of sable on a field of sable,
whereas the hens – three, four, five – in fashionable
yellow gum-boots, are meekly back from Harrods.
Once a year (tonight, perhaps) such virtue has its reward;

raising his eyes to heaven – as if about to commit hara-
kiri – the cock will hop on each in turn and, unhurri-
edly, do three or four push-ups,
reaching all too soon for a scuffed Elizabeth Bishop.

'Paul? Was it you put the *pol* in polygamy
or was it somebody else?' While their flesh is notably
    gamey
even in bilberry-time, their winter tack's
mainly pine-shoots, so they now smack

of nothing so much as turpentine.
Room 233. Through a frosted, half-opened
window I listen to the love-burps and borborygms of a
   capercaillie
('horse of the woods', the name means in Gaelic)

as he challenges me to mortal combat.
The following morning, Saint Joan has moved into the
   camp-bed.

Asra

The night I wrote your name in biro on my wrist
we would wake before dawn; back to back: duellists.

The Panther

For what it's worth, the last panther in Massachusetts
was brought to justice
in the woods beyond these meadows
and hung by its heels from a meat-hook
in what is now our kitchen.

(The house itself is something of a conundrum,
built as it was by an Ephraim Cowan from Antrim.)

I look in one evening while Jean
is jelly-making. She has rendered down pounds of
    grapes
and crab-apples
to a single jar
at once impenetrable and clear:
'Something's missing. This simply won't take.'

The air directly under the meat-hook –
it quakes, it quickens;
on a flagstone, the smudge of the tippy-tip of its nose.

Cauliflowers

Plants that glow in the dark have been developed through gene-splicing, in which light-producing bacteria from the mouths of fish are introduced to cabbage, carrots and potatoes.

The National Enquirer

More often than not he stops at the headrig to light
his pipe
and try to regain
his composure. The price of cauliflowers
has gone down
two weeks in a row on the Belfast market.

From here we can just make out
a platoon of Light
Infantry going down
the road to the accompaniment of a pipe-
band. The sun glints on their silver-
buttoned jerkins.

My uncle, Patrick Regan,
has been leaning against the mud-guard
of the lorry. He levers
open the bonnet and tinkers with a light
wrench at the hose-pipe
that's always going down.

Then he himself goes down
to bleed oil into a jerry-can.
My father slips the pipe
into his scorch-marked
breast pocket and again makes light
of the trepanned cauliflowers.

All this as I listened to lovers
repeatedly going down
on each other in the next room . . . 'light
of my life . . . ' in a motel in Oregon.
All this. Magritte's
pipe

and the pipe-
bomb. White Annetts. Gillyflowers.
Margaret,
are you grieving? My father going down
the primrose path with Patrick Regan.
All gone out of the world of light.

All gone down
the original pipe. And the cauliflowers
in an unmarked pit, that were harvested by their own
    light.

The Briefcase

for Seamus Heaney

I held the briefcase at arm's length from me;
the oxblood or liver
eelskin with which it was covered
had suddenly grown supple.

I'd been waiting in line for the cross-town
bus when an almighty cloudburst
left the sidewalk a raging torrent.

And though it contained only the first
inkling of this poem, I knew I daren't
set the briefcase down
to slap my pockets for an obol —

for fear it might slink into a culvert
and strike out along the East River
for the sea. By which I mean the 'open' sea.

Part Two

MADOC
A Mystery

[*Thales*]

When he ventured forth from the smallroom
he activated a sensor-tile
that set off the first in a series of alarms
and sent a ripple through Unitel.

He was running now. A frog
scrawled across a lily-pond.
A kind of hopscotch frug.
There'd be a twenty second

delay. Then he'd almost certainly succumb
to their cotton-candy
scum-foam.
He'd only to whisper 'In Xanadu . . .'

and smile 'did Kubla Khan . . .'
His voice-count
was still good. Then a retina-scan.
On the stroke of three the door opened

and all hell broke loose.
There were Geckoes armed with Zens
to either side. He let go of his old valise.
And since

there was nowhere to turn
he turned to the unruffled, waist-deep hedge
with its furbelow of thorns
and deckle-edged

razor-ribbon.
One or two Geckoes began to applaud.
He took the plunge. Whereupon
he became just another twist in the plot.

[*Anaximander*]

'Are you telling me that South was as free as a bird
to wander through the Dome
and it wasn't until he went to take a dump . . .'
'Then we knew something untoward

had happened.' 'How?' 'He weighed more rather than
   less
when he left the crapper.'
'Much more?' 'Exactly as much as the scrap of paper
we repossessed from his valise.'

[*Anaximenes*]

The Geckoes lowered their stun-guns
and looked askance

when an Omnipod
scuttled

along the scarp
of trifoliate Chinese orange

on which he'd whittled
himself down to size.

They could see this was no saniteam
but a wet-set

out for revenge.
They heard him scream

'The fluted cypresses rear'd up
their living obelisks'

as a whatsit
was clamped to his bod.

Then an oxygen-mask.
And, though one of his eyes

was totally written-off,
he was harnessed to a retinagraph.

[*Pythagoras*]

'It looked as if he'd simply xferred the motto
from the Roanoke Rood.'
'The which?' 'The Roanoke Rood or Rule.
A scorch-marked lump of wood

they found somewhere on the Outer Rink
at the turn of the century.
It's under a sheet of imaglass
in West 14.'

'Where South had limited right of entry.'
'Exactly. But other than this motto – "CROATAN" –
it was mud.'

'Until?' 'Until we discovered his gloss
in sympathetic ink:
C[*oleridge*] RO[*bert Southey The S*]ATAN[*ic School*].'

[*Heraclitus*]

So that, though it may seem somewhat improbable,
all that follows
flickers and flows
from the back of his right eyeball.

[*Parmenides*]

A woodchuck gets up on its hind legs and tail
to check the azimuth
and squinny
down the fork in the trail

where the Way of Seeming and the Way of Truth
diverge. He upsets
his own little tin pot and trivet
to tumble-pour

down the burrow
from which he derived.
September, 1798. What could be more apposite
than that into this vale

a young ass or hinny
bear Samuel Taylor Coleridge?
We see him reach
into his pantaloons for a small, sea-green vial,

then be overwhelmed by another pang of guilt.
A flock of siskins
or some such finches
blunders up from the Susquehanna.

Given the vagaries
and caracoles
of her star-gazing Narragansett colt
it's unlikely that Sara Fricker

will ever make good the yards, feet and inches
between herself and S.T.C. A grackle
blurts out from the choke-cherries.
The colt can no longer suppress a snicker.

[*Empedocles*]

The woodchuck has had occasion
to turn into a moccasin.

[*Anaxagoras*]

§

For a week now, since he came down with a fever,
Cornplanter and Red Jacket

have kept a vigil by Handsome Lake.
Sassafras. Elder.

Ewe's-milk.
They look at each other. They speculate

on whether his chest might be colder.
They press a rust-speckled,

jagged
glass to his mouth. It refuses to mist over.

§

In the light of the X Y Z affair
America and France are limbering up for war.

§

Near Femme Osage creek, on the lower Missouri,
Daniel Boone

comes on a beaver caught in two separate
traps.

It has gnawed both drubs
to the bone.

This beaver, like the woodchuck, is an emissary
from the Great Spirit.

[*Protagoras*]

At which Alexander Cinnamond, the Scots-
Irish scout,

unbuttons his saddle-holster.
He's undertaken to lead them to Ulster

for a keg of powder and a pair
of ear-rings. They're now half-way there.

De dum, de dum, de dum, de dum,
de dum, de dum, de dum, de dum.

Cinnamond fondles a tobacco-
pouch made from the scrotal sac

of a Conestoga who must, we suppose,
have meddled with the Paxton Boys.

He muses to himself
as he raises it to his mouth

and teases open its gossamerish thongs:
'Mon is the mezjur of all thungs.'

[*Zeno*]

Perhaps this was indeed a Seneca buck
whose low-pitched chortle

from among the choke-cherries
threw Sara into momentary

disarray.
A life-sized turtle

in red and yellow ochres
scram-

bles aimlessly about his torso.
When he goes to scratch his back

there's a quiver
of fully-fledged arrows.

By which time Sara will have recovered
her perfect equilibrium.

[*Socrates*]

§

While one by one the rest of the cavalcade
draw level
with her in the glade.
Her sisters, Edith Southey and Mary Lovell,

are astride a strawberry roan.
Their man-servant, Shad,
is driving a spanking-new, iron-
shod

wagon in which Lovell himself is laid.
Three days ago, a wood-sprite
worried his shoulder-blade.
The wound has begun to suppurate.

Messrs Allen, Burnett, Le Grice and Favell
dismount and pitch
the first of several
bell-tents. A pure-white spaniel bitch

runs rings round them. Cinnamond builds
a fire, helps Lovell to the shelter of a cairn
of stones and applies another poultice
of hemlock-bark and acorns.

§

A thrum of hooves. If Southey is to Bucephalus
as a flame is to its wick
then Southey is a flame.

He clutches a small, already-battered valise,
a sheaf of quills, a quire of vellum.
He cancels everything in his wake.

[*Leucippus*]

And in the twinkling of an eye
the weather-vane
swiggles at its own behest
and the chest

of tools, the great auger,
the plow-sock,
the sacks
of flour and sugar . . .

[*Democritus*]

The rip-saw, sundry axes,
some boxes
of sea-salt,
the cast-iron skillet,

the meal-ark,
the muddle of ropes
and barrel-hoops,
salted herrings, salted pork,

assorted helves and handles,
the tallow candles
and pewter
candle-sticks, the keg of powder,

the griddle,
the dozen-odd bags
of seed, the pearwood box
of tricks, the cradle,

the mahogany desk,
the cask
of rum, the bath with claw feet,
go smattering into the void.

[*Antisthenes*]

Coleridge follows a white spaniel
through the caverns of the Domdaniel.

[*Plato*]

My mother said I was mad; if so, she was bit by me, for she wished to go as much as I did. Coleridge and I preached Pantisocracy and Aspheterism everywhere. These are two new words, the first signifying the equal government of all, and the other the generalization of individual property; words well understood in the city of Bristol.

(Southey)

[*Diogenes*]

§

When Sara stretches into the dark
of the meal-ark

her hand is taken by a hand.

§

A tongue-in-cheek snail goes metic-
ulously across a mattock's

blade-end.

§

As Southey squats in the claw-foot tub,
oblivious of the shadow-rub

of horses against his tent.

[Aristotle]

Now, if you are in the mood for a reverie, fancy only
me in America; imagine my ground uncultivated since
the creation, and see me wielding the ax, now to cut
down the tree, and now the snakes that nestled in it.
Then see me grubbing up the roots, and building a
nice, snug little dairy with them; three rooms in my
cottage, and my only companion some poor negro
whom I have bought on purpose to emancipate. After
a hard day's toil, see me sleep upon rushes, and, in
very bad weather, take out my casette and write to
you, for you shall positively write to me in America.
Do not imagine I shall leave rhyming or
philosophizing; till at last comes an ill-looking Indian
with a tomahawk, and scalps me — a most melancholy
proof that society is very bad, and that I shall have
done very little to improve it. So vanity, vanity will
come from my lips, and poor Southey will either be
cooked for a Cherokee, or oysterized by a tiger.

(Southey)

[*Theophrastus*]

De dum, de dum, de dum, de dum, de dum.

[*Pyrrho*]

§

New York. In his closing remarks to the Wigwam
of the Order of Saint Tammany
the Republican mugwump,
Aaron Burr, alludes not only to *Timon*

and *Titus Andronicus*
but Milton
by way of Gray; he drinks
to the demise of 'mute, inglorious' Hamilton

and his Federalist chaff:
the Tammanyites respond with a grudging chorus
of 'Aaron, Aaron, Aaron . . .'

§

The spaniel ushers Coleridge along a path
covered with grass
to a belt of blue beads, a bow made of horn.

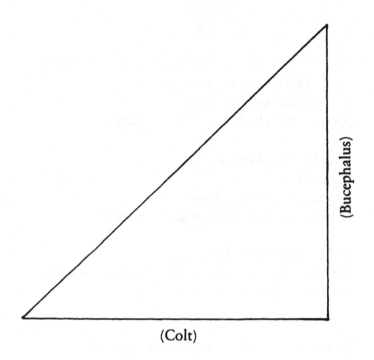

(Bucephalus)

(Colt)

[*Zeno*]

It had dawned on Shad that something was askew
when he went to draw and hew

and found, under the mottled porch
of a clump of birch,

the water spaniel, Cerberus,
her throat slashed like a silk-lined purse

and her eyes
wide-open, world-weary and oddly wise.

[*Epicurus*]

They tip
Coleridge into the icy tub

to bring him round.
His ornate

serge-de-Nîmes
vest and pantaloons

are laudanum-
mackled. His eyes a raccoon's.

He's coming to
his senses when a toe

stirs, then the right fore-claw,
and the tub begins to cla-

mber like an alligator
towards the birch-bower.

The spaniel reeks of elder-
flowers.

A length of tarred twine
dangles from a twig with (1)

a silver ear-ring
and (2) a salted herring.

[*Archimedes*]

Coleridge leaps out of the tub. Imagine that.

[*Aenesidemus*]

We doubt even that we doubt. Why on earth
would Cinnamond, if Cinnamond
it was, abduct one of the 'milliners of Bath'?
Unless, of course,

she did go willingly. If not,
why no ransom-note?
How could Sara so readily
abandon Berkeley and Hartley?

What are we to make of Bucephalus
striking out due north,
the colt
and a pack-horse

due west? In any case, both
trails are already cold,
both almost certainly false.
It remains to be seen what they have in mind.

[*Seneca*]

§

A woman falls to earth, on to the muddy turtle-back
of the earth.

§

There Wind has his way with her, and leaves her two
arrows as tokens, one untipped, one tipped with flint.

§

Her sons are Flint and Sapling.

§

Wherever Sapling runs, trees leap up behind him.
Whenever he throws a handful of earth, living things
rush off in all directions. Each winter, the animals are
impounded by Flint in a cave of ice. In spring, Sapling
sets them free.

§

Sapling makes two-way rivers for easy canoe-journeys.
But Flint undoes the work, causing rivers to flow,
like this, in one direction only.

§

And the river flows into Handsome Lake.

[*Dionysius*]

Who hears his name called by each of three angels.
They are wearing skunk bonnets.
Their jowls
are daubed with lamp-black and vermilion paint.

[*Epictetus*]

I carried Epictetus in my pocket till my very heart was ingrained with it, as a pig's bones become red by feeding him upon madder.

(Southey)

[*Ptolemy*]

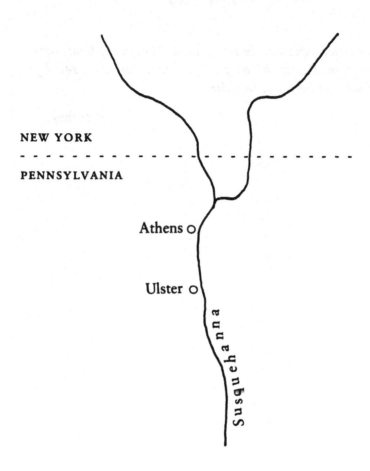

[*Galen*]

It transpires that Bucephalus is even now
pumping a jet
of spunk into the rowdy-dow-dow
of some hoity-toity little skewbald jade.

[*Origen*]

A tavern in New Orleans. John Evans drains a glass of
    port:
'It seemed to me that the Omaha chief, Blackbird,
though he fed his enemies arsenic,
was a gentleman like yourself.' His companion in the
    snug

is Brigadier-General James Wilkinson,
on whose behalf he raised the Spanish ensign
over the Mandan villages:
'That the Mandans are Welsh is, then, fallacious?'

Evans agitates his dregs:
'They're no more Welshmen than Spaniards,
though time and time again I watched them geld

a yearling colt
with a rawhide lanyard
and a sherd of flint. No, No more Welshmen than
    Turks.'

[*Plotinus*]

§

The next morning, before they pass under
the mare's tail of a waterfall

where the Way of Reason
narrows to the Way of Faith,

Coleridge and Southey must pause
to draw lots. They wave

to Shad and the rest of their tearful,
much-depleted garrison,

who'll try for Ulster at their own pace
before the onset of winter.

§

Shad waves back, and bends for the mattock
he'll use to dig

a grave for the dog
when it comes to him in a flash — MADOC.

[*Augustine*]

May, 1799. The hamlet
of Carthage, New York, into which he has stumbled,

is constantly raided by Senecas.
The only street is a glorified mud-sink

which Southey is about to ford
when he recognizes the star on the forehead

of a shaggy-coated Bucephalus,
who points him in the direction of an ale-house.

[*Proclus*]

Might Allen and Favell be discussing metaphysics
as they lean on their bill-hooks?

They've already girdled
five acres of trees to make way for the cattle

and razor-back hogs.
Hartley frolics with one of the young Cayugas

who frequent the gate
of the stockade.

Her name is Bean. Her sisters are Corn and Squash.
The only sound is the swoosh

of a bull-roarer.
Favell spits in his palms: *Laborare est orare.*

[*Pseudo-Dionysius*]

In a second vision, Handsome Lake meets his favourite
    dog,
one of many

he saw fit to sacrifice
in last New Year's white dog ceremony.

It carries its own head, like a crest,
between its paws. It wags

its tail in recognition, springs up and licks his face.
Handsome Lake also meets Jesus Christ.

[*Benedict*]

Southey takes its tongue between finger and thumb
and the door-bell is struck dumb, de dum.

[*Boethius*]

So furious are their grunts and groans, so fierce the
   blizzard
from a cedar-
bole they're cutting into shakes and studs
Shad and Le Grice have missed the clippety-clop of a
   letter

for Edith.
As she comes running out to them, the blade
of the rip-saw gives a last spasm
and struggles free. In the shored-up chasm

of the saw-pit, Shad begins to contemplate
one crinkled saw-tooth
as if everything depends on it. He's in such a lather

of sweat and blood and sawdust
that he might easily be mistaken for some kind of satyr
or wood-wizard.

[*Scotus Eriugena*]

We can discern, through the tobacco-fug,
Cinnamond ensconced at a bench
with a stoneware jug

of punch
and a bowl of stew
before him. The floor's a midden

into which he might at any moment spew
potatoes, onions, carrots, mutton.
'What,' he riddles himself, 'is the difference

between an Irishmon and a puddle?'
When a voice pipes up, 'The bottle . . .'
Cinnamond frowns

in disbelief, then squawks and squalls
as Southey rams the sheaf of goose-quills
into his eyes.

[*Avicenna*]

'From his brimstone bed at break of day
a-walking the Devil is gone
to look at his snug little farm the Earth
and see how his stock went on . . .'

[*Anselm*]

De dum, Te Deum, de dum, Te Deum, de dum.

[*Abelard*]

The letter from Sara to Edith Southey's
stamped with her seal, a coronet

and the legend *TOUJOURS GAI*;
on a snig of hemp

or linsey-woolsey's
hung a teeny-weeny key;

and a message in her own *Lingo Grande*:
'Signifump. Signifump. Signifump.'

[*Averroes*]

§

'He went into a rich bookseller's shop.
Quoth he, We are both of one college
for I sat myself like a cormorant once
hard by the tree of Knowledge.'

§

Though he's now encumbered by two jennets
laden with pelts
Southey fairly jaunts
through the woods, humming a little ballad.

§

'As he went through Cold Bath Fields he saw
a solitary cell . . .'

[*Maimonides*]

§

'And the Devil was pleased for it gave him a hint
for improving the prisons of . . .'

§

Coleridge stops in his tracks. A Seneca
wearing only a breech-

clout
and a skunk

bonnet and cradling an arquebus
has just stepped out

from behind a beech.
Coleridge is genuinely perplexed.

He unclasps and dabbles
in the portmanteau

for which Southey and he drew lots.
He brandishes John Eliot's

Algonquian bible
and quaveringly intones the name of 'Manitou'.

§

The Mohawk, as he turns out to be, goads
and bullies

him through the gateless gates
of Canada

and into
the formal gardens and unfathomable fountains

of this, the summer palace
of the Old Man of the Mountains.

[*Fibonacci*]

Up a spiral staircase with precisely two hundred and thirty-three steps, each conjured from the living rock.

[*Bacon*]

Through the hoopless hoop of a black rainbow.

[*Aquinas*]

To the room where Thayendanegea, Joseph Brant,
appears to him as in a dream,

his head shaved but for a scalp-lock
adorned with a white

feather, his bearskin
robe, his shirt a calico

print
set off by a solid brass

gorget, his sword-stick with its brass ferrule.
He offers Coleridge tea and scones,

pres-
erves and clotted cream.

He folds his arms: 'Would
you say you came here of your own free will?'

[*Duns Scotus*]

Southey has wedged himself between two boulders
by the side of a creek.
His pine-cone fire splutters
out. Bucephalus speaks to him in halting Greek:

'This is indeed a holy place
dedicated to the sun god, Bel.'
Southey can but dimly make out the blaze
on his poll:

'Were the secret of the ogam
script on the edge of this standing stone
known to the Reverend Samson Occom
he would hold it in disdain.

Yet his own people, the Mohegan,
are the seed of the Celtic chieftain, Eoghan.'

[*Occam*]

One or two things we should know about Joseph Brant.

He was born in 1743, the son of a ginseng-gatherer.

His name means 'two sticks tied together'.

In the spring of 1761 he received a good conduct medal from George the Third for his services against the French.

He studied Hebrew, Latin and Greek at Wheelock's Academy, now Dartmouth College.

In 1776 he visited London, where the King presented him with a Masons' apron. He was interviewed by James Boswell for *The London Magazine*.

He sided with the British during the Revolutionary War.

In 1797 he dined with Aaron Burr and his daughter, Theodosia, who considered serving him a human head.

Though he is nominally 'King of the Mohawks' he is plagued by schisms.

Five years ago his son, Isaac, tried to kill him.

This past winter a strangled white dog was slung from a pole just outside Brant's Town.

This is enough to be going on with.

[*Buridan*]

Since Bucephalus is neither more nor less
inclined
to the grey jennet's
shy come-hither

than the chestnut's
blatantly swollen gland
(not to speak of the cross
on her withers)

he'll dilly-dally
and dawdle and dither
until he's utterly
at a loss

as to the whys and wherefores
of either or either or either or either.

[*Wycliffe*]

Another thing. In 1786 Brant again visited London. He met with the Archbishop of Canterbury to discuss his new edition of the Mohawk Prayer Book.

[*Mandeville*]

It moulders now in the double-dusk
of the valise
along with a copy of Voltaire's
L'Ingénu: cowries,

hooks-and-eyes, hawks'-bells;
a matching pair
of conchs;
more roanoke; pig-tails

of tobacco; such bagatelles
as the hank
of Washington's hair
so prized by Thomas Poole;

the apothecary's
array, tsk tsk,
of red and violet and blue phials
and philtres.

[Brant]

§

When George Burnett climbs
to his thirty-foot-high look-out
post he surveys six cabins caulked
with moss and lime

and the clinkered roof
of their new barn.

§

The ten-year-old Lord Byron
stamps his cloven hoof.

§

The sword-stick. Its brass ferrule.
'Did you come of your own free will?'

§

Apart from a leak of yellow
from the nail-shop
where Shad is slowly turning a felloe
everything's ship-shape.

[*Erasmus*]

Twelve months ago they embarked, de dum, Te Deum,
on a merchantman out of Rotterdam

and were seen off from the Bristol quay
by a bemused citizenry

including Hucks and Cottle, their fellow-
Pantisocrats, who now dismissed the plan as folly.

They would anchor briefly in an Irish harbour
to take on board the usual raparees

and rapscallions;
cattle, pigs, sheep and, of course, the stallion.

[*Machiavelli*]

Bucephalus gives Southey a knowing look:
'It appears that Shadrach Weeks is in league
with Cinnamond, while Cinnamond is in league
with the Seneca prophet, Handsome Lake.'

[*Copernicus*]

Te Deum. De dum. Te Deum. De dum. Te Deum.
An omnium-gatherum
of stoats
and weasels and other vermin

got up in ermine
or swallow-tail coats
and armed with shillelaghs
and spiked clubs

come at a gallop
through the valley.
When the leader's mount gives way under him,
de dum,

he lights a fire at the critical point
just behind its belly-band.

[*More*]

§

It's a year to the day since Thomas Jefferson
tabled his first version

of 'the mould-board
of least resistance' for a plow

to the American
Philosophical Society.

§

A year, too, since the Unitedman, the MacGuffin,
paid a Dutch captain one hundred guilders

and took passage on a coffin-
ship from Westport.

MacGuffin has now changed his name to 'Smith'.
He is in the service of Aaron Burr.

§

Little does Jefferson know, as he saddles the Morgan
and slopes off down to Mulberry Row

and the less-than-smooth
furrow of his light-skinned Jocasta,

that 'Smith' overhears them link and uncouple.
Little does he think that the world is out of kilter.

[*Luther*]

I was haunted by evil spirits, of whose presence,
though unseen, I was aware. At length an arm
appeared through a half-opened door, or rather a long
hand. I ran up and caught it. I pulled at it with
desperate effort, dragged a sort of shapeless body into
the room and trampled upon it, crying out the while
for horror.

(Southey)

[*Scaliger*]

Southey awakes from the nightmare to a hurricane
of hooves, though barely within earshot;

at this distance, not even Bucephalus can reckon
if they're (1) shod or (2) unshod;

he nonetheless strains for effect on his halter:
'*Eadem*, de dum, *sed aliter*.'

[*Paracelsus*]

What wouldn't Coleridge give for a tipple-tope
of the celebrated Kendal Black Drop?

[*Calvin*]

Back on the hill, at Monticello,
a chill

runs down Minerva's spine;
the door of the laundry's

open.
She grips her lantern.

Already scared out of her wits
by the demoniacal

chuckles from the vats,
the involuntary creak of a mangle,

she happens on a bar of lye-soap
and the name **********.

[*Ascham*]

From behind a freshly-scraped, buffalo-hide arras
on which hangs an elk-horn

bow and a brangle of blood-stained arrows
a woman begins to keen:

'Now your snouterumpater is a connoisorrow
who has lost her raspectabilberry.'

An elk-horn bow. A brangle of blood-stained arrows
tipped with chalcedony and jasper.

[Dee]

*The historical facts on which this poem is founded
may be related in a few words. On the death of Owen
Gwyneth, king of north Wales, AD 1169, his children
disputed the succession. Yorwerth, the elder, was set
aside without a struggle, as being incapacitated by a
blemish on his face. Hoel, though illegitimate, and
born of an Irish mother, obtained possession of the
throne for a while, till he was defeated and slain by
David, the eldest son of the late king by a second wife.
The conqueror, who then succeeded without
opposition, slew Yorwerth, imprisoned Rodri, and
hunted others of his brethren into exile. But Madoc,
meantime, abandoned his barbarous country, and
sailed away to the west in search of some better
resting-place. The land which he discovered pleased
him: he left there part of his people, and went back to
Wales for a fresh supply of adventurers, with whom he
again set sail, and was heard of no more.*

(Southey)

[*Scaliger*]

As he goes to emend a jotting on the flyleaf
of a small, morocco-bound tome,
Southey plucks a grey goose-quill from the sheaf;
its nib is stiff with grume, de dum.

[*Brahe*]

Once his mast inclines towards the forest
the star in the bucket
from which Burnett slakes his thirst . . .

[*Bruno*]

Is momentarily out of true. At the picket,
the alchemy
of horses. A mallet-tap on a spigot.

Not so much as a glimmer
from the nail-shop. Then the cut and thrust
of a double-edged claymore.

[*Hakluyt*]

A room over the New Orleans tavern.
John Evans rummages in his lice-ridden shirt
and unfolds a chart
of a river wider than the mouth of the Severn.

Beyond the Mandan
villages, beyond this squalid
ruck in the quilt,
is yet another range of mountains.

There, surely, are the tell-tale
blue eyes and fair skins
of the scions
of the prince of Wales

for whom Evans has searched in vain.
About his neck is hung
a bag of asafetida, or 'devil's dung'.
He bares his arm. The physician gropes for a vein.

[*Bacon*]

A black slave wearing one white glove
opens
a copper chafing-dish.
A boiled
ham studded with cloves.
Broad beans.
Brant is at once outlandish
and polite:
'Only last winter
I went out to stuff a chicken
with snow
so it wouldn't spoil.
I caught an ague
for my trouble. I took it as an omen.
I remembered Cornelius Sturgeon
hacked
to death by his own Onondagas.
He, too, had stuffed himself with whiteness.'
'What of this white woman
in Cornplanter's
Town? Is she British or American?'
'I know
only that her name is Sybil
and that she belongs to Red Jacket.
I know nothing of her origins.
This I swear to you, as God is my witness.'

[*Galileo*]

§

The Mohawk braves take off their skunk bonnets.
Other than a statue of the Good Twin

carved from a twenty-foot log
they can see little of Cornplanter's Town,

what with its pall of smoke like a scab
on a wound. Coleridge crawls to his vantage-point.

§

When he squints through the telescope
given to Brant by Lord Sydney

in 1786, he suddenly knows all he needs to know:
nailed to the statue is a white dog.

[*Campanella*]

An island on the Ohio
where Harman
Blennerhassett
is building a Roman
villa
complete with mosaics
and frescoes
and a modest cupola.

The bog-oak
lintel
was unearthed
on his god-forsaken
family estate
in Kerry.
He had it shipped
from Philadelphia
by barge
and bullock-cart.

It took a dozen
men to hoist
it into position.
One was cut in half,
eheu,
when the cable
of the windlass
snapped.

Blennerhassett studies
a marble
bust of himself
above the hearth.
It's ever so slightly
awry.

That rather unsightly
stand
of birch
and sugar-maple
is destined
soon to become a lawn.

An artesian
well. A lily-pond.
The sound of Handel's
Water Music
on a spinet
or harpsichord.
A peacock
and a dappled fawn.

This is The New Atlantis.
The City of the Sun.

[*Kepler*]

Which is already burning off the fogs
and marsh-gas
from the glen. The halloo of a fox.
The report of geese

from the Lac
Qui Parle. Southey begins to prime
a flint-lock.
A snatch of the now-familiar rhyme:

'An apothecary on a white horse
rode by on his vocation
and the Devil thought of his old friend
Death, in the Revelation.'

[*Boehme*]

What a beautiful thing it is, in a pot, urine.

Has Coleridge somehow given Shad offence
by treating him, de dum,
as a mere factotum?

Why do those blue beads, the bow made of horn,
remind him not of Sara, but Mary Evans?

[*Harvey*]

Just as he's ramming a wad into the pistol
Southey has the uncanny . . .

a black pustule
or blood-blistereen

roughly the size of a guinea
has erupted on the stallion's pastern.

[*Hobbes*]

§

Coleridge can no more argue from this faded blue
turtle's splay
above the long-house door to a universal
idea of 'blue' or 'turtle'

than from powder-horns, muskets,
paddles, pumpkins,
thingums, thingammies,
bear-oil against mosquitoes,

hatchets, hoes, digging-sticks,
knives, kettles,
steel combs, brass tacks,
corn-husk masks or ceremonial rattles

to anything beyond their names. The silent drums.
The empty cask of trade-rum.

§

While the white woman is being rogered
by one Seneca tipped with chert

she sap-
sips

a second.
Coleridge turns away, sickened,

snaps shut the telescope
and fumbles for his pony's halter-rope.

[*Descartes*]

§

In 'France', a little child, a limber elf,
pulls a straw bee-skep over himself.

§

Now doubting everything but his own doubt
Southey bites on a weevil-riddled
ship's biscuit
and goes in search of the Pantisocrats.

[*More*]

Though he's self-evidently a leprechaun
who barely comes up to the ankle

of Lord Moira (or the waist
of Lady Donegal)

all London hails
the self-evidently angel-voiced

Tom Moore as the new Anacreon.
This includes the *other* Prince of Wales.

[*Pascal*]

Jefferson is so beside himself with glee
that he finishes off a carafe

of his best Médoc;
his newly-modified polygraph

will automatically
follow hand-in-glove

his copper-plate 'whippoorwill'
or 'praise' or 'love':

will run parallel to the parallel
realm to which it is itself the only clue.

[*Boyle*]

Before Coleridge has had time to settle
into the saddle
a hunting-party gallops
up through the hickories.

The hides
of the ponies are smeared
with mud from the Allegheny.
Cornplanter's son, Henry O'Bail,

is resplendent
in a cougar-
and-lynx-
skin vest, red leggings

and stove-pipe hat.
Were it not for the Quakers,
Swayne and Simmons,
bringing up the rear

he might well appeal
to his tomahawk.
Just as he's about to vent
his spleen

his bedraggled pony breaks wind
so vehemently
it shakes the rafters
of the metaphysical long-house.

All collapse
in helpless laughter.
This horse-fart smells of newly-cut grass
and, is it nutmeg?

[*Locke*]

Not until he sees the great cloud-eddy
renewing itself in a pond
will Southey have even the faintest idea
of what's happened.

Until he hears
the sobbing of a resinous plank
that's already been shaved of its ears
his mind's a total blank.

[*Spinoza*]

Brother, I rise to return the thanks of this nation to our ancient friends — if any such we have — for their good wishes towards us in attempting to teach us your religion. Perhaps your religion may be peculiarly adapted to your condition. You say that you destroyed the Son of the Great Spirit. Perhaps this is the merited cause of all your troubles and misfortunes.

Brother, we pity you. We wish you to bear to our good friends our best wishes. Inform them that in compassion towards them we are willing to send them missionaries to teach them our religion, habits and customs. Perhaps you think we are ignorant and uninformed. Go, then, and teach the whites. Select, for example, the people of Buffalo. Improve their morals and refine their habits. Make them less disposed to cheat Indians. Make the whites generally less inclined to make Indians drunk and to take from them their lands. Let us know the tree by the blossoms, and the blossoms by the fruit.

(Red Jacket)

[*Burnet*]

Dangles
by one fretful ankle
over the illustrious dung-hill.

As to holding forth
on the inherent worth
of the earth,

he would surely be on the brink
of speech – were it not for the brank
of his own prong.

[*Hooke*]

O spirochete. O spirochete. O spirochete.

[*Malebranche*]

Notwithstanding his having a whiff
of a stake burned at the stake of itself
like a lithe and lissome Joan of Arc.

Notwithstanding his having a taste
of tar-water and a sooty crust
Southey will stay completely in the dark.

[*Newton*]

Until it strikes him, as if by some fluke;
this strict, unseasonable, black snowflake.

[*Burnet*]

Te Deum. Te Deum. Te Deum. Te Deum. Te Deum.

[*Leibniz*]

Which falls a little too patly into the scheme
of things. It now seems inevitable,
for example, that the pivotal beam
of the barn will topple

at any moment, making a splash
of orange, while the ghosts of individual
log-cabins step, naked, from their ash-
pink farthingales and fiddle

with their hair. Bucephalus hobbles
through what was meant to be the best
of all possible
worlds, hitches himself to a hitching-post

and arches his neck:
'Since we're now approaching the gates of Hell
you should know that the "nock" in Mount Monad-
    nock
is indeed the Gaelic word *cnoc*, a hill.'

[Bayle]

§

The last thing he remembers is the arc
of his pony's tail

skittering off like a comet
as his own unkempt

head dashes against a rock.

§

It turns out that Henry O'Bail

has had Coleridge and his few belongings
thrown into a rude palanquin

and all conveyed, at a frantic lick,
to Cornplanter's Town, and Handsome Lake.

[*Vico*]

A hand-wringing, small, grey squirrel
plods
along a wicker

treadmill that's attached
by an elaborate
system of levers

and cogs and cranks
and pulleys
and gears

and cams and cinches
and sprags and sprockets
and spindles

and tappets and trundles
and spirochetes
and winches

and jennies and jiggers
and pawls
and pranks

and the whole palaver
of rods
and ratchets

to a wicker
treadmill in which there plods
a hand-wringing, small, grey squirrel.

[*Toland*]

Nutmeg. A sizar at Jesus. The smell of laver-bread
    reveals
Coleridge lying with Mary Evans in the Gog Magog
    Hills.

[*Mandeville*]

§

The buffalo-hide arras covers the filthy smoot
of a bee-hive hut.

§

A gopher mimics from its honeycomb:
'Where's my stumparumper? Where's my sillycum?'

[*Clarke*]

Then consoles itself, in the waste of alkali,
with a sprig of the as-yet-unnamed *Clarkia pulchella*.

[*Berkeley*]

That treadmill might have existed only in the mind
of a child, were the child not now a non-entity
under his flower-strewn, almost-imperceptible mound:
BERKELEY COLERIDGE 1798–99

[*Butler*]

Try as Southey may to reconcile himself
to a whimsical

whirligig going unscathed
while Burnett unravels

from his gibbet,
while Berkeley and Lovell

have met their ends,
he's set upon by, of all things, a sheaf

of corn, by some flibbertigibbet
wielding, in one hand,

a rusty sickle
and, in the other, the sned of a scythe.

[*Voltaire*]

CORNPLANTER

It goes without saying that Cinnamond
sold her to the Crees, with whom he's made a pact.

HIGGENBOTTOM

And this?

HANDSOME LAKE

A liniment
of aspen and hawk-weed
for your scalp.

HIGGENBOTTOM

I would be swayed less by your herb tisanes
and juleps
than by your offering me a dozen
warriors who know the ways of the Crees.

RED JACKET

It goes without saying. But you must earn
our trust.

HANDSOME LAKE

I see a path covered with grass.

HIGGENBOTTOM

A belt of blue beads. A bow made of horn.

[*Hartley*]

Southey's about to blow out the goblin's brains
when the bee-skep
slumps forward to divulge
his three-year-old nephew who escaped,

supposedly, to 'France'.
Four days ago, he determines,
Hartley had stayed with Edith, Shad and Burnett
while the others left for the village

of Athens. There came
ten or twelve men with pails of burning pitch.
They burned and burned.
Uncle Shad went into the fiery furnace

to save the strawberry roan.
Then an angel rescued *him*.
An angel? The angel looked like 'Cindermans',
though he also looked like Daisy.

(By this he must mean the border collie
with one eye-patch.)
Aunt Edith? She, too, has fled to 'France'.
Southey follows him through the smoke

to the shallow gully
overgrown with horse-tail ferns
where he finds Edith, dazed,
wearing only a crumpled, blood-spattered smock.

[*Franklin*]

That teeny-weeny key. Bear it in mind.

[*Reid*]

§

None of this impinges as yet on Private Moses Reed.

§

In spite of various qualms and cavils
Coleridge has deemed it the lesser of two evils
to present Handsome Lake with the valise.

§

'At any moment now, the retina will disintegrate.'

[*Hume*]

September, 1799. They're putting the finishing touches
to the maze of dykes and ditches
beyond the live-oak palisade.
The stone blockhouse is proof against a mortar-blast.

Its roof is of ten-inch-thick sheets of slate
hauled here by mule-sled.
For a weekly ration of grog and a few gew-gaws
Southey has enlisted fifteen disaffected Cayugas.

One of whom guards Edith. She rolls over in her
  hammock
and twiddles a newly-peeled, sharpened osier
from the bundle by her side. A hummock

under her chemise. Its occasional jitter-jolt.
Her recurrent dream of a shorn and bloody hawser.
And, as always, Bucephalus, niggling: 'Who *owns* the
  child?'

[*Frederick the Great*]

September, 1800. A Cayuga wet-nurse dandles
the infant in her lap
while Southey recites from his endless
saga of *Thalaba*

The Destroyer: 'the fluted cypresses
rear'd up
their living obelisks . . .'
Hartley sulks as Bean expresses

milk from her diddly-doos,
then resolutely cups
the spout of his tortoise-shell powder-flask:
'Not until you see the whites of their eyes.'

[*Rousseau*]

December, 1802. The two Toms, Jefferson and Paine,
look out through the silver birches,
past undulating spruce and pine,
to the illimitabilities of the Louisiana Purchase.

[*Diderot*]

In the downstairs study, Jefferson's aide-de-camp
makes a tally of blankets, hats and gloves;
opium, laudanum,
cinnamon, oil of cloves;

marlinspikes, wimbles,
gimlets and awls;
needles and thimbles;
fish-hooks; powder and ball;

the theodolite, quadrant, compass and chain . . .
Except for his not as yet having got
to grips with the code

based on the key word 'artichokes',
all's set fair for his clandestine mission.
Meriwether Lewis swaggers up and out to the jakes.

[*Putnam*]

'Not until you see the whites of their eyes.'

[*Smith*]

A small gust of wind through the open window.
A gasp on a cello or viola.
A flittering across the portfolio
Lewis has left untied.

A cursory glance
at the ledgers and log books.
Abracadabra. Hocus-pocus.
A thumb through a well-thumbed Linnaeus.

Until, among bills-of-lading and manifests
and almanacs and a Mercator
plan of the heavens,

this: the map drawn up by John Evans
that shows such a vast
unsulliedness the very candle gulps and gutters.

[*Kant*]

April, 1804. It stands to, well, 'it stands to reason'
that Wilkinson, who's 'in the pay of' Spain,

should 'sow the seeds of treason'
in the 'fertile mind' of Aaron Burr,

of whom Alexander Hamilton holds 'a despicable
  opinion'.
The tedium, de dum, of it all. The slurry-slur.

[*Burke*]

The Envoy Extraordinary and Minister Plenipotentiary
of His Britannic Majesty,

one Anthony Merry
(though 'merry' is hardly *le mot juste*)

laboriously
presents Tom Moore, late of Bermuda,

to Jefferson, the sublime and beautiful, the paragon
of civility, who prompt-

ly turns on his heel and shuffles off in his slippers,
unwittingly slighting the leprechaun.

[*Darwin*]

§

Independence Day, 1804. The moment-of-dawn salute
from the swivel-mounted howitzer
in the stern of the flat-boat
sends up a cloud of parakeets.

Though this barquette
draws only three feet of water
it has more than once foundered in the silt
and quicksand of the river-bed.

§

Clark scrutinizes the newly-repaired cordelle
that caught on a submerged tree-trunk.
It's spliced and greased.
Sergeants Pryor and Ordway dispense two gallons

of whiskey. None for Hall or Collins
(both flogged for being drunk)
or the slave, York, who dances a bear-quadrille
to the scraping of Gibson and Cruzatte.

§

By mid-afternoon, a series of sawyers and snags.
Labiche and Shields
have capsized the white pirogue.
It looks as if Floyd may have dysentery.

Meanwhile a sentry,
one of the brothers Fields,
has been bitten by a rattle-snake.
Lewis dresses the wound with nitre and boiled bark.

§

Then strides out behind Willard's makeshift smithy
among cocklebur and wild timothy.

[*Priestley*]

§

On the western branch of the Susquehanna,
Putnam Catlin's

intent on guddling
a trout.

§

Only when she's in her last agony
does the trout renege

on a silver ear-ring
and cough it up and spit it out.

§

It lies on the floor of the birch-bark canoe.
Catlin's all of a sudden filled with dread.

[Watt]

Coincidentally, as she charges his porringer
from a piggin of steamed milk,

Edith skites
his immmmmmmmmmmmmmmmmmmmmmmaculate

pea-green waistcoat;
this is much more than Southey can endure.

[*Paine*]

Exactly a week later, on the banks of the Hudson,
Burr sends a ball through the kidneys

and milty spleen
of Alexander Hamilton.

A blood-trump out of Hamilton's mouth.
Burr's whisked away by William Van Ness and 'Smith'.

[*Saussure*]

§

August 7th. Lewis has sent a hunting-party
in search of the deserters, Moses Reed and La Liberté.

§

August 11th. The Captains mull
over the tumulus or mole

where the Omaha chief, Blackbird,
was buried

on his white war-horse.

§

August 18th. Reed's brought back and forced

to run a gauntlet of ramrods
and switches. Boils and buboes. Haemorrhoids.

§

August 20th. Floyd dies of colic and melancholia.

§

August 25th. His spirit clambers up the holy

Mound of the Little People, to the moans
of its thousands of eighteen-inch-high demons.

§

October 14th. John Newman is sentenced to seventy-five
lashes for having uttered a mutinous oath.

§

October 25th. Though the sandstone bluffs and spurs
give way, for the most part, to sparsely-

wooded, deeply-fissured mesas
redolent of wormwood, of the artemisia's

turpentine and camphor,
there's still the occasional, delicately-chamfered

column of honey- or salmon-coloured querns
surmounted, as here, by an obsidian cornice.

Camphor and turpentine. Elk-slots. Bear-scats.
Drouillard and Shields, the scouts,

can see directly across the stately saraband
of the Missouri to the corresponding

scumble of mosques and minarets
and the three-hundred-odd Mandans and Minnetarees.

[*Jefferson*]

Has today received (1) a live gopher (2) a magpie (3) a
piece of chequered skin or hide and (4) a cipher that
reads . . . 'A-R-T-I-C-H-O-K-E-S'.

[Bentham]

§

In fancy now, beneath the twilight gloom,
come, let me lead thee o'er this 'second Rome',
this embryo capital, where fancy sees
squares in morasses, obelisks in trees.

§

October, 1804. A secret letter from Merry to Burr
encloses these lines by Tom 'Little' Moore:

§

The patriot, fresh from Freedom's councils come,
now pleased retires to lash his slaves at home;
or woo, perhaps, some black Aspasia's charms,
and dream of freedom in his bondsmaid's arms.

§

Merry's seal is of ivory set in jade
and reads, predictably, ΙΑϽ ƧЯUO⎰UOT.

[*Maimon*]

Amidst oohs and ahs and clucks and cackles
the Mandan girls take turns to wet
their fingers and rub the charcoal
from what must be York's underlying white.

[*Godwin*]

Needless to say, these are not girls but berdashes
who beckon him into their earth lodge
near a maelstrom

of brood mares; York follows the stream
that back-breakingly portages
itself from ledge

to ledge, past beehive huts, a sweat-house,
a flotilla of bull-boats
(buffalo-

hides on ribs of willow)
to where Joseph Whitehouse,
the Irishman, Gass, and the German, Potts,

have so fortified themselves on dried smelt
and salmon
they're in ecstasy:

to the hub of the Mandan village, the wooden hogshead
containing their most treasured amulets
and secret talismans.

[*Wollstonecraft*]

February 11th, 1805. Sacajawea nibbles at the quirt of her newly-born's umbilical cord.

[Cooper]

Strong evidence has been adduced that Madoc reached America, and that his posterity exist there to this day, on the southern branches of the Missouri, retaining their complexion, their language, and, in some degree, their arts.

(Southey, Preface to *Madoc*, April 1805)

[*Schiller*]

May 5th, 1805

We set out verry early and had not proceeded far before the rudder Irons of one of the Perogus broke which detained us a short time. Potts gave Capt Lewis to know that we are follied by a man on a Spotted horse. The Countrey on both sides is as yesterday handsom & fertile. The river rising & current strong & in the evening we saw a Brown or Grisley beare on a sand beech. I went out with one man Geo Drewyer & killed the bear, which was verry large and a turrible looking animal, which we found verry hard to kill. We Shot ten Balls into him before we killed him, & five of those Balls through his lights.

(Clark)

[*Fichte*]

This very morning, a sixty-foot sloop
was seen to put in
at the Island. The dunt
of a light skiff

against the jetty.
While Aaron Burr
mesmerizes his host
with the barbel

of an Idea,
the ubiquitous 'Smith'
hovers about the pier.
He's absorbed by the dent

below his own water-line. A purple
tick-bite no bigger than a button.
Burr raises his glass to Blennerhassett:
'Syllabub. Syllabub. Syllabub.'

[*Malthus*]

I am startled at the price of Madoc. In fact, books are now so dear that they are becoming rather articles of furniture than any thing else; they who buy them do not read them, and they who read them do not buy them. I have seen a Wiltshire clothier who gives his book-seller no other instructions than the dimensions of his shelves. If Madoc obtain any celebrity, its size and cost will recommend it among those gentry – libros consumere nati *– born to buy quartos and help the revenue.*

(Southey)

[*Hegel*]

William Labiche and the boatman, Cruzatte,
ruminate

on a ten-foot-long buffalo-
gut

coiled
between them, its listless, puce

and amethyst
cloud-

remnant
sporadically a-shiver.

They've already gorged on the raw
liver

laced
with gall and gun-powder.

Each takes an end. And they grumble-
gripe

through the slick
shambles

(*Ametas*
and Thestylis

Making Hay-Ropes)
until

it's all but lost its
slack

and they're locked in a putter-
buss

stalemate.
So these brave fellows

draw
their bone-handled

knives.
The Bitterroot Valley. September, 1805.

[Smith]

Madoc *is doing well; rather more than half the edition is sold, which is much for so heavy a volume. The sale, of course, will flag now, till the world shall have settled what they please to think of the poem. The* Monthly *is all malice, and is beneath all notice; but look at the* Edinburgh, *and you will see that Jeffrey himself does not know what he is about. William Taylor has criticised it for the* Annual *very favourably and very ably. Taylor has said it is the best English poem that has left the press since* Paradise Lost; *indeed, this is not exaggerated praise, for, unfortunately, there is no competition.*

(Southey)

[*Coleridge*]

Labiche and Cruzatte will put up their blades
when an Appaloosa

comes rollicking past in a blur of tricorn
hat and epaulettes

and twill unmentionables
and shrugs off the erstwhile Light Dragoon,

Silas Tomkyn Comberbache,
as though he's one dapple less on her back.

[*Mill*]

The five-year-old goes truffling with the hogs
and plants an acorn in his mouth.

Southey prestidigitates the key
on its snig of hemp or linsey-woolsey

while Bucephalus goes down on one knee:
'Penguin. From the Welsh

pen and *gwynn*, meaning "head" and "white".'
An infusion of charlock

and jimsonweed.
He tugs his forelock:

'As for the white-headed boy under the oaks
you know he's not a Southey. He's a *South*.'

[*Schelling*]

September 5th, 1805

*We assembled the Chiefs & warriers and Spoke to
them with much dificuelty as what we Said had to pass
through Several languages before it got into theirs,
which is Spoken much thro the throught.*

(Clark)

*These natives have the Stranges language of any we
have ever yet seen. They appear to us as though they
had an Impedement in their Speech.*

(Ordway)

*These Savages has the Strangest language of any we
have ever Seen. They appear to us to have an
Empediment in their Speech or bur on their tongue.
We take these Savages to be the Welch Indians if their
be any Such.*

(Whitehouse)

[*Herbart*]

§

While they deliberate on the Flatheads' 'gurgle'
and 'brogue'
Lewis and Clark have him confined to the coracle
at the stern of the red pirogue

§

where Coleridge spies a Croton bug or beetle
making its regal
progress along a paddle.
The water will suddenly give him back a gargoyle

§

with Southey's eyes and mouth. A sniff of aloes.
The iceberg-
bellows, the bleats and brays of a great battle.
The crumble-itch of a periwig.

§

Then, just as suddenly, a child in blue and yellow
creeping unwillingly to Christ's Hospital.

[*Gauss*]

§

The first watch is taken by John Potts
and Patrick Gass,

who seems infatuated with an abacus
of turquoise beads.

§

In St Louis, Burr asks General Wilkinson
to calculate

the cost, in gold,
of an ordnance of two hundred cannons.

§

Coleridge is given his measure of taffy
along with a mash of various

kinds of berry
and the roots of *Lewisia rediviva.*

[Davy]

In Sweden a very curious phenomenon has been observed on certain flowers, by M. Haggern, lecturer in natural history. One evening he perceived a faint flash of light repeatedly dart from a marigold. From the rapidity of the flash, and other circumstances, it may be conjectured that there is something of electricity in this phenomenon.

(Coleridge)

[*Byron*]

Again stamps his cloven hoof
as he conjugates the verb 'to have'.

[*Schopenhauer*]

§

'And where did you come by the Nez Percé pony?'

§

Coleridge absentmindedly ties a knot
in the waist-cord of his breeks.

§

'Are you with the Northwest or X Y Companies?'

§

Retina. From the Latin *rete*, a net.

§

'When I struck the "c" from *castor*
I found myself in the company of John Jacob Astor.'

§

In the waist-cord of his breeks
he inextricably tightens the knot.

§

'Billet him with Newman in the red pirogue.'

[*Hamilton*]

September 7th. Might the spectre of Hamilton
playing a *schottische*

on his melodeon

of blood and guts and shit and piss
have been just enough to give Wilkinson pause?

[*Faraday*]

'Tis said, in Summer's evening hour
Flashes the golden-colour'd flower
   A fair electric flame:
And so shall flash my love-charg'd eye
When all the heart's big ecstasy
   Shoots rapid through the frame.

               (Coleridge)

[*Comte*]

§

Coleridge and Newman have poled their unwieldy dory
up a fast-flowing, narrow tributary.

§

While Gass and Potts slept the sleep of the just
they ransacked the medicine-chest

for calomel, bee-balm
and what little was left of the opium.

A compass and binnacle.
Brooches, bangles

and other knick-knacks.
A Sheffield knife. A calumet. Some kinnikinnick.

§

With first light, they manhandle the red pirogue
on to a sand-bar and throw up a wind-break

of cottonwood boughs. Coleridge wants simply to verify
the opium. Five grains. Tusk. Tongue furfurry.

[*Newman*]

Would seem to have taken another about-turn
and shown a clean pair of heels. Why, though, had he
  drawn

the knife? It lies point-upward near a flint, a punk
and a pile of kindling on the sandy bank

where he must have been meaning to build a fire
and where his footprints, see, where they, see, disappear.

[Emerson]

Plotinus, a man memorable for corrupting philosophy, was in favour with Gallienus, and requested his royal highness would give him a ruined city in Campania, which he might rebuild and people with philosophers, governed by the laws of Plato, and from whom the city would be called Platonopolis. The design would certainly have proved impracticable in that declining and degenerate age – most probably in any age – yet I cannot help wishing the experiment had been tried; I could rhapsodise most delightfully upon this subject, plan out my city, the palaces and hovels of Southeyopolis.

(Southey)

[*Feuerbach*]

§

The tinkle
of an Aeolian harp.

Eels.
Elvers.

An inkle
of black crêpe.

§

His pirogue
reels

through a sulphurous
brook.

§

What if Coleridge were to plait
a geyser's

cobalt-
azure

into a less than ideal
rope whereby

to wheedle-
warp

himself into the well, well, well
of his own fontanelle.

[*Mill*]

Hartley and South have created something of a stir
by dropping a rooster
down the flue
of his study. Rather than fling an ink-well

at the devil,
Southey corners it in the ingle-
nook
and unceremoniously wrings its neck.

Rather than haruspicate
its gizzard
for some portent of disaster,

rather than haggle with Zoroaster,
he looks to Bucephalus, who will hazard
only that *Madoc* means 'the greatest, greatest good'.

[Darwin]

*Set out early proceeded on up the Creek passing
through a Small glade at 6 miles at which place we
found a horse. I derected him killed and hung up for
the party after takeing a brackfast off for our Selves
which we thought fine.*

(Clark)

[*Kierkegaard*]

§

Lewis and Clark have split up, the better to track
Newman and the British spy, Comberbache.

§

In Monticello, the snaggle-toothed gopher
tries his paw at the polygraph.

§

As he takes a skelly at the massive gantry
that now dominates the rath,
Bucephalus finds himself in yet another quandary
as to either or either or either or either.

§

Hartley and South spin a teetotum, de dum, de dum.

[*Boole*]

§

Coleridge is now resigned to the fact that Sara
could be anywhere west of the Missouri.

§

Henry O'Bail has had the icon of the Good Twin
dismantled and dumped in the Allegheny,
though not before sawing off the narrow plank
on which he stands: 'assimilation'.

[*Thoreau*]

September 20th, 1805

We had proceeded about 2 miles when we found the greater part of a horse which Capt. Clark had met with and killed for us.

(Lewis)

[*Marx*]

§

In the Northwest Company post on the Assiniboine,
among bags of flour and bricks of marchpane

and bolts of none-so-pretty and nankeen
and barrels of whiskey garbled with laudanum,

§

a trade-mark fox
cocks an ear from its rifle-stock

§

at the faint de dum, de dum
of the Crows, perhaps, up to their old shenanigans.

[*Foucault*]

Even as Southey ponders the variables in torque
on the counter-weight and derrick

of the great ballista
he cannibalized

from that vividly-imagined
sky-machine's

wheels within wheels,
Bucephalus hints at the livid welts and weals

on his such-and-such:
'You're already under siege

from within, just as these blenny-blebs and blets
are storming my Bastille.'

[*Spencer*]

The trading-post; a gelding hitched to the hitching-rail
and a palfrey hitched to the gelding's tail.

The palfrey's saddle; a fowling-piece; its scrimshandered
mother-of-pearl inlay: a salamander.

[*Pasteur*]

The gelding's apishamore, meanwhile, is a languid,
crimson mackinaw blanket.

[*Kelvin*]

Southey rests on a wannigan. Cams and cinches.
Sprags and sprockets.
Parakeets.
Finches.

Wrens and whimbrels.
Tups and wethers.
Laverocks. Leverets. Levers.
Tumbrils.

Tricoteuses and sans-culottes.
Red-shanks. Her spackled cambric.
Ox-head. Dithyrambic.
Tups and wethers. Boars. Sows. Gilts.

The pike and carnelian sturgeon
that will rise to this, as to every, occasion.

[*Huxley*]

*I set out early and proceeded on through a Countrey
as ruged as usial. At 12 miles decended the mountain
to a leavel pine Countrey. Proceeded on through a
butifull Countrey for three miles to a Small Plain in
which I found maney Indian lodges, but fiew men a
number of women & children. They call themselves
Cho pun-nish or Pierced Noses. Their diolect appears
verry different from the flat heads, altho origineally the
Same people.*

(Clark)

[*Maxwell*]

A tittle-tattle of light on his ax.
Sackbuts. A butt of sack.

The butt of malmsey.
St Elmo's

Fire. Fata Morgana.
Gomeril. Regan.

Will-o'-the-wisp. Jack-o'-lantern.
The seas incarnadine.

Cochineal. Cinnabar. Cinnamond.
Ruby. Rubicon. Rubicund.

The rail. The grouse. The gudgeon.
His escutcheon

is a buckler or targe
of goatskin over staves of larch.

[*Butler*]

On which Southey has blocked out an inverted chevron
and a pair of gryphons

rampant, blue on grey;
they unfurl a pennant with, so far, the letters 'CRO—'.

[Brentano]

We had proceeded about two and a half miles when we met Reubin Fields whom Capt. Clark had dispatched to meet us with some dryed fish and roots that he had procured from a band of Indians.

(Lewis)

I found Capt. Lewis & the party Encamped, much fatigued & hungery, much rejoiced to find something to eate of which they appeared to partake plentifully.

(Clark)

The pleasure I now felt in having tryumphed over the rockey Mountains and decending once more to a level and fertile country where there was every rational hope of finding a comfortable subsistence for myself and party can be more readily conceived than expressed.

(Lewis)

[*Mach*]

November 3rd. Bucephalus
is now so at odds with himself

his very stones
keep their distance.

He's completely engrossed
by the rosettes

and ribbons
on his tumid, de dum, Dick Turpin.

[*Popper*]

Beyond the ramparts, a Cayuga grips
the heft of a rattle
made from the carapace
of a mud-turtle.

The jaws
of his poplar-wood false face
are the jaws
of a vice.

The tongue prates
from its garrotte.
The neb is the neb of a prie-dieu
or misericord.

One eye is a wizened fern-
pod,
the other a fat gold sovereign
to airie thinnesse beat.

Its ogle-leer. Its wry perusal
of a field
of mangel-wurzels. A parasol
of horsehair and felt.

The Cayuga adjusts the lambda
of his grotesque
helmet
and grips the rattle-heft, tsk tsk.

[*Putnam*]

§

As he reads aloud to the boys from *Thalaba*
Southey closes his right
eye and removes a tiny piece of grit
from the eyelid. A finger-flick. A fillip.

§

'Any moment now. The retina. Disintegrate.'

§

This detail will hardly be lost
on Putnam Catlin's nine-year-old, George,
so irresistible in his urge
to sketch Southey on a skiffle of slate.

[*Peirce*]

§

As the weeks have gone by, Coleridge feels less
　　squeamish
when he finds a blue and yellow grub
in a raw bulb of quamash.

§

However long he maggots upon why the crop
of mangolds should suddenly spoil,
Southey is none the wiser.
He orders them plowed under. Goody-good for the soil.

§

Pike, pickerel. Hog, hoggerel.
Cock, cockerel. Dog, doggerel.

§

Beyond the ramparts, the False Face lifts his visor.

[*James*]

The pile of horse-dung at the heart of Southeyopolis
looks for all the world like a dish of baked apples.

[*Hartmann*]

§

Coleridge is about to quench his
thirst in an alkali-

tainted pool. An exorbitant,
harum-scarum

head
over his shoulder.

§

Helter-skelter
across the lava-beds.

§

The almost invisible scrim
of a rabbit-net

strung across a gully.

§

From the Latin, *rete*. Unconscious.

[*Nietzsche*]

It seems that nothing – be it arsenic or leeches
or an impromptu sweat-lodge

rigged up from an old bell-tent
at one end of the stable – nothing's of any dint

to the stallion, he's so shot-through, so spangled
with the cankers and carbuncles

of syphilis.
Three nights ago, Southey lay down with Bucephalus

and blew in his ear, as if he might fan the embers.
He's held him since in a fast embrace.

[*Cantor*]

§

The word on the Burr-Blennerhassett cabal?
Quibble, quibble, quibble.

§

With such innnnnnnnnnnnnnnnnnnnnnnfinite
tenderness, such care,

Southey brushes the glib
from behind the stallion's ear

and takes aim,
de dum. A flash in the pan. A thunder-clap.

Blood-alphabets. Blood-ems.
A babble of blood out of the broken fount.

[Bradley]

Great joy in camp. We are in view of the Ocian. This great Pacific Octean which we been so long anxious to See. And the roreing or noise made by the waves brakeing on the rockey Shores (as I suppose) may be heard distictly.

(Clark)

[*Edison*]

§

Coleridge has fallen in with a band of Modocs
who extemporize a sudatory

from the overturned dory.
They ply him with such mild emetics

as yarrow and Oregon
grape. He's tantalized

by the all-pervasive tang of dulse
or carageen.

§

That night the Modocs light a greasewood beacon
and repeatedly sound a conch.

§

The morning brings a party of Spokanes.
Their chief offers Coleridge the use of his wife

in exchange for (1) the kinnikinnick
and (2) the Sheffield knife.

[*Bell*]

Brant's Town. A communiqué
from Theodosia Burr

to her old friend, the King of the Mohawks.
Brant invites 'Smith'

to stay for supper,
throughout which he swigs

brandy from the mouth
of a nacreous

skull he took somewhere near Fort Stanwix.
Or was it Niagara?

[*Sorel*]

Southey clears a space on his escritoire
for the bundle of osiers

and the ax;
the teeny-weeny key: the pearwood box.

[*Frege*]

The Spokane chief still wants to dicker
for the knife, on the blade of which are etched

the initials 'G' and 'R';
Coleridge has now assumed the name 'George Rex'.

[*Meinong*]

§

Inside the pearwood box — hold on a minute —
is an exact replica

of the valise.

§

Its very contents are identical.

§

Down to the hooks-and-eyes, hawks'-bells,
the not-quite-matching pair

of conchs,
the selfsame hank

of Washington's hair
so prized by Thomas Poole.

§

(Southey peers out at the block
and tackle

with which Bucephalus
was this morning lowered into his mound.)

§

All except for a dog-eared letter in cuttle-
ink addressed by Coleridge to 'my dearest Cottle'.

[*Royce*]

First Allen; then Le Grice; Hartley and Mary Lovell:
one by one, they've grown disenchanted.

Now, without so much as a 'by your leave'
or a 'begging your pardon'

(though true at least to his name), Favell
has taken the chestnut jennet

and set out for God-knows-where. The ever-loyal Edith
busies herself in the herb-garden.

[*Freud*]

Her recurrent dream of a shorn and bloody hawser.

[*Saussure*]

Nothing in this could have prepared him for
the bleached tarpaulin

stretched over stays of baleen
where the Spokane woman slinks from the fur

of a sea-otter
and sways before him like a ship's figurine.

His eye is going against the grain
of her weatherbeaten cedar

when, by a blubbering lamp, Coleridge divines
a heart-shaped tattoo

on her left teat
and a Cupid's dart from, this can't be, EVANS.

[*Husserl*]

July 4th, 1806

*This being the day of the decleration of Independence
of the United States and a Day commonly scelebrated
by my Country I had every disposition to selebrate this
day and therefore halted early and partook of a
Sumptious Dinner of a fat Saddle of Venison and
Mush of Cows (roots). After Dinner we proceeded on
about one mile to a very large Creek which we
assended some distance to find a foard to cross. Altho'
the debth was not much above the horses belly, the
water was so strong it passed over the backs and loads
of the horses.*

(Clark)

[*Bergson*]

A sennet of hautboys. The glint
of afternoon sunlight on the panoply of hauberks and
  halberds.
An ungainly colonnade
of Cayugas. Chimeras and camelopards

on their antique
livery. Southey's own tunic is of saffron
and indigo,
his cape the fell of a wolverine.

Since he's suffering from a mild case of the flux,
he's couchant on a tavelin
of vairs and minivers. In his right hand is the valise,
in his left a three-tined javelin

with which he admonishes, from his litter,
the Cayuga so slovenly as to have dropped his muzzle-
  loader.

[Dewey]

July 29th, 1806. Aaron Burr entrusts a certain Samuel Swartwout with a letter for General Wilkinson. This letter is written in three ciphers: one hieroglyphic, another based on a specific edition of *Entick's Pocket Dictionary*, the third an alphabet cipher devised by Wilkinson and 'Captain Smith'.

[Whitehead]

§

Southey wakes in a cold sweat;
penguins don't have white heads.

§

April, 1797

My dearest Cottle,
        *I am fearful that Southey will begin
to rely too much on story & event in his poems to the
neglect of those lofty imaginings that are peculiar to,
& definitive of, the* POET.

S.T. Coleridge

[*Santayana*]

The weary statesman for repose hath fled
from halls of council to his negro's shed
where blest he woos some black Aspasia's grace
and dreams of freedom in his slave's embrace.

(Tom 'Little' Moore, *Epistles, Odes and Other Poems*)

[*Schiller*]

Hawk-nosed, with a hawk's clumsily seeled eye,
duodenum, de dum, de dum,
Cinnamond fastens the palfrey's reins
to his gelding's tail.

His wrinkled breeks
are of stuff you might take for shagreen.
He's breakfasted on an oatmeal bannock
or scone.

He tilts the whiskey bottle
at Shad, at the featureless, frank, smoked ham
of Shad's face. O for a flitch of salty
pork.

Nothing. Cinnamond coaxes the bung
into the bottle and yanks
at his loose-fitting, shalloon-lined galligaskins:
'Mon is the mezjur of all thungs.'

[*Unamuno*]

This latest jibe sends Jefferson into such a rage
as to make the Guelphs and Ghibellines

seem tame. The gopher chittering from its cage:
'We must have Favell in Favell alone.'

[*Croce*]

§

Southey has just overseen the flogging of the Cayuga,
whose yelps resound through the delirium
as echo-echoes.

§

No wonder Cinnamond's trews are so very becoming;
they're made from the epiderms, de dum,
of at least four, maybe five, hapless Gros Ventre women.

[*McTaggart*]

Although Burr has suffered a blow – *O tempora, O
    mores* –
in the recalling of Anthony Merry

and the unlikelihood, now, of British support,
we find him in quite exuberant spirits.

This may have to do with the fact that a brig
laden with one hundred barrels of pork

is already making its way up-river
to Blennerhassett's Island. It's now. It's now or never.

[*Rutherford*]

The scalp on Cinnamond's saddle-horn
had belonged to a Crow
whose skull he would bombard
with a stone club.

As he'd worked a broken sabre
from temple to temple
and under the sodden divot,
didn't your man leap

to his feet
and begin to run
through the bushes, balancing a caber

of gore,
and leaving behind the greater part
of his wimple.

[*Russell*]

In the *Edinburgh Review* of July 1806, Moore is categorized as 'a public nuisance' and 'the most licentious of modern versifiers', to which he takes grave exception. Had this happened only a few years later, he would almost certainly have asked Lord John Russell to assist him on the field of honour.

[*Lovejoy*]

§

August 14th. The ever-hospitable Mandans
don their buffalo-bull
head-dresses and dance a Buffalo Dance
to celebrate the return of the Captains.

§

Edith hooks a cedarwood pail
to the windlass
over the well and lets go of the capstan.
A headlong, clanking plummet. Relentless.

§

September 23rd, 1806

*Set out decended to the Mississippi and down that
river to St. Louis at which place we arrived about 12
oClock. we Suffered the party to fire off their pieces as
a Salute to the Town. we were met by all the village
and received a harty welcom from it's inhabitants.*

September 26th, 1806

a fine morning we commenced wrighting &c.

(Clark)

[*Moore*]

In the meantime, 'Little' and Francis Jeffrey
of the *Edinburgh Review*

will have met at Chalk Farm for a duel.
In as long as it takes their seconds to load

their pistols ('How do you tell a Scot
from a sot?')

these arch-rivals
have become the best of friends

and, in the end, as they say, 'in the end
common sense prevails . . .'

Which is just as well, since Jeffrey's pistol
is found to be short of its bullet.

[*Marconi*]

§

October 8th, 1806. Swartwout finally delivers the cryptogram to Wilkinson: 'Our object, my dear friend, is brought to a point so long desired. The gods invite us to glory and fortune. It remains to be seen whether we deserve the boon.'

§

October 20th. Wilkinson informs Jefferson of the conspiracy. The President issues warrants for the arrest of Burr and Blennerhassett.

[*Jung*]

§

Bear-claws; a soap-stone frog; two big-horn fleeces
sewn into their own rumens;

of all the totems, de dum, that might assuage
the Mandan gods, none will speak more eloquently

from the hogshead-shrine than this: this swatch
of a crimson mackinaw blanket.

§

Southey has now proscribed (1) the white dog ceremony
and (2) the society of False Faces.

[*Einstein*]

December 11th, 1806. When the Wood County militia
led by Colonel Phelps
come at full gallop
across the Island, one breaks his neck, *eheu*,

on a ha-ha.
The jangle of a bayonet
across the spinet.
There's neither hide nor hair of Blennerhassett.

While his men slaughter and roast
a milch-
cow in the ruins

of the garden,
the Colonel pores over a rune
on the bog-oak lintel. Is it 'CROATAN' or 'CROATOAN'?

[*Hartmann*]

November 24th, 1807. During yet another squantum
of boiled ham and beans, the skull begins to drink

from the astonished mouth of the King
of the Mohawks, inveigling him into its kingdom.

[*Schlick*]

In years to come, he'll run his hands like quannets
over the Contessa's

breasts and thighs while Douglas Kinnaird
looks on admiringly and strokes his yard.

For now, we may put *Hours of Idleness* down to Byron's
lack of – might one surmise? – 'experience'.

[*Neurath*]

§

New Year's Day, 1809. At a literary *fol-de-rol* in
  Edinburgh
Jeffrey's introduced to the bankrupt, exiled Burr,

now travelling under the aegis of Jeremy Bentham.
'Jeremy . . .?' '*Bentham*'; the name is lost in the pande-
  monium.

§

Josiah and Thomas Wedgwood's annuity to the Panti-
  socrats
is unexpectedly cut. 'Any moment now. Disintegrate.'

§

March 1st, 1809. In *English Bards and Scotch Reviewers*
Byron launches a fierce

attack on the 'ballad-monger' Southey and Tom Moore
who, as we know, is not one to demur

from inviting him over to Chalk Farm,
whence (yet again) they return as brothers-in-arms

to drink each other's health from (yet again) a human
  skull;
Southey henceforth dubs them 'The Satanic School'.

[*Lewis*]

October 11th, 1809. Governor Lewis attempts to cram
the gralloch-grummle
back into the hole in his belly.
The half-ounce ball
from a second heavy-calibre
pistol has clabbered
his brow, leaving part of his brain exposed
to the idle boast
that, since these were his own weapons,
he must have acted himself, and was not acted upon.

[*Ortega*]

August 10th, 1815. In the course of a game of lacrosse
played in his honour

by the Seneca élite,
Handsome Lake takes a firm hold

of the handle of his valise and sets out on an inner
journey along the path covered with grass.

[*Herrigel*]

Through the hoopless hoop of an elk-horn bow.

§

To the Northwest Company post
on the Assiniboine, which is even now beset

by a war-party of Crows.
Their war-chief (that *éminence grise*

in the buffalo rug)
is William Clark's old freed-man, York.

§

While his warriors are gainfully employed
in breaking out barrels, bales and bolts,

York keeps harking back to the mile-high
column of smoke in an otherwise flawless sky.

[*Bachelard*]

Six hours ago, and twenty miles away, they had chanced
on a wagon drawn by a mule-team,
de dum,
and driven by a grizzly bear

who levelled his smooth-bore
not at them, but Shad,
and finished him off with a single shot.
He then stood his ground as, one by one, the Crows

charged at him in an elaborate criss-cross
only to cajole
him with their coup-crooks and cudgels.
When York swooped down and caught him by the scruff

of the neck, Cinnamond simply sloughed off
his skin and slithered
under the wagon like a lizard.
Then, as if this might indeed hold them at bay,

he lit a whisper of hay
and set fire to a semi-circle of sage-brush
that shortly engulfed the wagon, where he surely
    perished.
York's throat still rankles with aniseed.

[*Bohr*]

He has nothing to show for his morning's exertions
but this caparison
of stuff he still takes for shagreen
and the one-eyed cloud on the distant horizon.

[*Baird*]

§

September 26th, 1820. At Femme Osage, on the lower
  Missouri,
Daniel Boone is about to give up the ghost

when the beaver-skeleton on the wall
starts to glow and hum, looks about to make sure the
  coast

is clear, then drags itself, traps and all,
across the floor, along the bed: 'Put me out of my
  misery.'

§

None of the paeans and panegyrics
trouble Southey so much as the 'Byron' of Byron, New
  York.

[*Collingwood*]

An even more distressing thought. On August 23rd, 1805, Lewis and Clark had submerged their boats, weighting them with stones, and were travelling on horseback when they met the Flatheads. How might Coleridge have stolen a pirogue, when there was none to steal?

[*Wittgenstein*]

'Now your stumparumper is a connoisorrow who has lost his raspectabilberry.'

[*Heidegger*]

'I wanted merely to assure you that the name 'Evans'
is akin to both 'Eoghan' and 'Owen

Gwyneth', the father of Madoc,
and that Madoc himself is, above all, emblematic

of our desire to go beyond ourselves . . .'
A tousle of loam

from the mausoleum:
'When my own grandsire, another Bucephalus,

surged through a fetlock-bracing creek
at the head of the force led by Partholan the Greek

and shook himself out on that Irish strand
he was confident, too, that his time was at hand.'

[*Gramsci*]

Coleridge casts a paternoster into the murky stream.
He himself has only a remote

idea of his whereabouts.
A communal hut. A remuda

of skeletal ponies. Rabbits and more rabbits.
Try as he may, he has but a dim

recollection of why he might have cut
these wind-chimes

from a cloudy, yellow lump of agate
and strung them like icicles

in the thatch. Still no take
on the line. He opens a rabbit-skin satchel

and starts to hoke
for a buddy-bud-bud of his so-called 'Paddy Nostrum'.

[Carnap]

§

February 6th, 1822. Byron is on his hands and knees
as he sookies another canto of *Don Juan*
into the daylight, by its nose;
he himself is his own ball-and-chain.

§

Of all men, saving Sylla the Man-slayer,
  Who passes for in life and death most lucky,
Of the great names which in our faces stare,
  The General Boon, back-woodsman of Kentucky,
Was happiest amongst mortals any where;
  For, killing nothing but a bear or buck, he
Enjoyed the lonely, vigorous, harmless days
Of his old age in wilds of deepest maze.

§

The Contessa, meanwhile, is taking a snooze;
a little dribble down her chin
is the only sign of their earlier antics
when she winkled the 'semen' out of 'semantics'.

[*Benjamin*]

Later that afternoon, or the next, a filibegged Byron will
    hobble
through the streets of Pisa
and trip over a cobble.
As he sprawls there, a group of boys
begin to jeer, '*Diavolo*'.
That night, he writes to Southey to propose
he either retract the 'Satanic' canard
or give him satisfaction. (This missive's intercepted by
    Kinnaird.)

[*Huxley*]

§

Bearing only his rabbit-skin satchel, five hawks'-bells,
the sacred

calumet,
a smidgin of laver-bread,

Coleridge is himself the blossom in the bud
of peyote.

§

Betimes a cormorant, betimes a white coyote,
will guide

him across the Lava Beds,
the Klamath

mountains, over plains and forests, to the ziggurats
of Southeyopolis.

[*Bakhtin*]

Where the flossofer
declaims

from Byron;
Coleridge remarks on the glair-

glim
of mica and feldspar

on the collar
of Southey's closely-knit byrnie.

[*Marcuse*]

He had written praises of a regicide;
   He had written praises of all kings whatever;
He had written for republics far and wide,
   And then against them bitterer than ever;
For pantisocracy he once had cried
   Aloud, a scheme less moral than 'twas clever;
Then grew a hearty antijacobin –
Had turn'd his coat – and would have turn'd his skin.

(Byron, *The Vision of Judgement*)

[*Lewis*]

Coleridge lays a comforting hand on Southey's shoulder.

[Gadamer]

He had sung against all battles, and again
*   In their high praise and glory: he had call'd*
Reviewing 'the ungentle craft', and then
*   Become as base a critic as ere crawl'd –*
Fed, paid, and pamper'd by the very men
*   By whom his muse and morals had been maul'd:*
He had written much blank verse, and blanker prose,
And more of both than any body knows.

(Byron, *The Vision of Judgement*)

[*Ryle*]

§

A twitch at his sleeve. Southey grasps the arm
and, with all his might,
wrangles the fiend across the room
and jerks its face into the candlelight.

§

Three Cayuga women are sorely vexed
by the sight of a phantom hound –
too small for a wolf, too big for a fox –
scrabbling near the stallion's burial-mound.

[*Lacan*]

The wraith pokes its tongue in Southey's ear –
'Rhythm in all thought, and joyance everywhere' –
before leaving only a singe on the air.

[*Tarski*]

§

The truth is that the phantom hound
was a coyote

the Cayuga women had killed with their bare hands
and tied by its brush to the postern-gate.

§

Southey interprets this as a revival
of the white dog ceremony

and inaugurates a witch-hunt.

§

May, 1826. Catlin steps back from his remarkably
    accurate
portrait of the Seneca orator, Red Jacket.

§

Blennerhassett bumps into Sam Favell:
'Sorry, Sam.' 'You must be Harman.'

'So *this* is the famous chestnut jennet?'

§

Southey draws a circle with his goose-quill pen
around the name of the wet-nurse, Bean.

[*Hook*]

§

Whom he sentences to twenty strokes of the birch.

§

After ten, her back and buttocks are blood-
smirched.

§

When he attempts to intercede on behalf of Bean,
South takes a blow to his shoulder-blade
for his pains.

§

The rod cuts right through his leather cuirass,
leaving a deep, trifoliate
graze.

§

The Cayugas are now openly in revolt;
that evening, South leads an exodus
through the dykes and ditches and into the shadows.

[*Popper*]

We last see him crouching in blood like a jugged hare.
As to where he goes? It's a matter of pure conjecture.

[*Adorno*]

§

April 19th, 1824. On the shore at Missolonghi
Byron's ball-and-chain is missing a link.

§

Independence Day, 1826. A gasp on a cello
or viola reverberates through Monticello.

The polygraph at its usual rigmarole.
The gopher pining for a caramel.

§

Jefferson clutches a bar of lye-soap
on which is scratched the name BEELZEBUB.

[*Sartre*]

June, 1830. As he follows General Clark from the main
    street
of St Louis and down a muddy path
Catlin is suddenly distraught.
Outside a booth

stacked with jiggers and jeroboams
of a patent elixir
based on tincture of opium,
a crowd has gathered

round a quack
and his guy, who has just now bitten the head
off a live pullet.

Something about this geek
reminds Catlin of his childhood.
A tiny piece of grit in the eye. The blebs. The blenny-
    blets.

[*Goodman*]

*Now I am inclined to believe that the ten ships of
Madoc, or Madawc, made their way up the Mississippi
and, at length, advanced up the Missouri to the place
where they have been known for many years past by
the name of the Mandans, a corruption or
abbreviation, perhaps, of 'Madawgwys', the name
applied by the Welsh to the followers of Madawc.*

(Catlin)

[*Arendt*]

September, 1832. Among these Mandan and Minnetaree
sachems and seneschals

who crowd around Catlin's easel
is one chief's daughter, Midday Sun;

her quaint medicine-
bag was taken during a raid on the Snakes:

as was the snig
of hemp about her neck and, yes, the miniature key.

[*Beauvoir*]

'Where's my stumparumper? My confabulumper?
My maffrum? My goffrum? My swarnish pigglepow?'

[Merleau-Ponty]

A few miles from Floyd's Bluff, we landed our canoe and spent a day in the vicinity of Blackbird's Grave. This very noted chief had been placed astride his horse's back, with his bow in his hand, and every warrior of his band painted the palm of his right hand with vermilion, which was stamped on the milk-white sides of his devoted horse. This all done, turfs were brought and placed around the feet and legs of the horse, and gradually up to its sides, and over the back and head of the unsuspecting animal, and last of all, over the head and even the eagle-plumes of its valiant rider, where altogether have smouldered and remained undisturbed to the present day.

(Catlin)

[*Quine*]

July 25th, 1834. A tinkle on an Aeolian harp
across the scrub

and salt-flats.
Coleridge props himself up under a canopy of gnats

and returns their call to a pair of chickadees:
'Quiddities. Quiddities. Quiddities.'

[*Lévi-Strauss*]

Since there's . . . since there's no kelp, come lettuce
draw back the flimsy rattan
lattice.

'At any moment now, his retina
will disintegrate.'
The burden

of a hurdy-gurdy
played by one Modoc damozel.
Another proffers him a sweet gourd

from her camisole.
Liver-wort. Bladder-wrack. Sea-kale. Samphire.
Elm. Holm-oak. Mistletoe.

Ash. Beech. Sycamore.
Yew; his self-bow backed with bone and sinew
in the belly of which the sagamore

finds a tiny crysal. Coleridge insinu-
ates himself through this crack into the vaults
of the Domdaniel. His familiar is a coyote made of snow.

[*Weil*]

'For the only society I have left now
is Bumble-Cum-Tumble and Doggy-Bow-Wow.'

[*Ayer*]

September 14th, 1836. Burr is incontrovertibly dead.

[*Austin*]

Even though the tree-girt auditorium,
de dum,

is deserted but for a troop
of nymphs and gnomes

and nixies,
Southey hikes up his tabard

and mounts the podium,
de dum.

As he warms to a diatribe
against his enemies

he nags
at the filigreed scabbard

of his sword
so as to emmmmmmmmmmmmphasize his words.

[Ricoeur]

For more than half a century, English literature had been distinguished by its moral purity, the effect, and in turn the cause, of an improvement in national manners.

A father might, without apprehension of evil, have put into the hands of his children any book which issued from the press, if it did not bear, either in its title-page or frontispiece, manifest signs that it was intended as furniture for the brothel.

This was particularly the case with regard to our poetry.

It is now no longer so, and woe to those by whom the offence cometh. The school which they have set up may properly be called the Satanic School; for though their productions breathe the spirit of Belial in their lascivious parts, and the spirit of Moloch in those loathesome images of atrocities and horror which they delight to represent, they are more especially characterized by a Satanic spirit of pride and audacious impiety, which still betrays the wretched feeling of hopelessness wherewith it is allied.

(Southey)

[Camus]

June 16th, 1837. The Mandan villages are ravaged by smallpox.

[*Grice*]

November 16th. The last word on Edith Southey's lips is 'sentiment'.

[*Barthes*]

March 20th, 1843. An almost naked 'Mandan' in
    harlequin
red and black lozenges
manages only one shot from his squirrel-gun
before a raiding-party of 'Shoshones'

rush his buffalo-wallow
and wrestle
him to the ground. His ululations are to no avail.
They take his scalp. The rehearsal

ends with the 'Shoshone' chief returning the pony-tail
wig to his victim
who stuffs it into a buckskin medicine-bundle,
his *vade mecum*,

which is then lodged in a glory-hole
back in his caravan.
This afternoon finds 'Catlin's Indian Gallery'
somewhere in deepest Wales. In the port, say, of
    Carnarvon.

[*Strawson*]

The 'Shoshone' is indisputably the artist's nephew, Theodore 'Burr' Catlin. As for the 'Mandan', when he washes off the lamp-black and vermilion paint, there's a fleur-de-lys on his shoulder-blade.

[*Franklin*]

§

And those teeny-weeny keys on their toggles
of hemp?

§

And those teeny-weeny keys on their toggles
of hemp?

§

Again, exactly identical.

[*Gass*]

In that buckskin parfleche decorated with porcupine
   quills
are item, a 'catlinite' pipe, item, a soapstone urn,
item, a belt of blue beads, item, a bow made of horn,
and item, de dum, de dum, Blackbird's and his horse's
   skulls.

[*Foucault*]

March 21st, 1843. A volley
of grape-shot from two foul-mouthed basilisks
or culverins.
A breach in the live-oak bailey.
Gavelocks. Pole-axes.

In 'France',
a False Face lifts his visor
and looks agog
from the horse-tail ferns
at the capstan's shorn and bloody hawser.

One Cayuga's
ganched on the teeth of a harrow.
Brays. Bleats. Bellows. Burning brands.
Bucephalus kicks
out in his long barrow.

A bloody handprint
on the flank
of the spirit-steed.
The stone blockhouse has borne the brunt
of the onslaught by a phalanx

of the Turtle clan, who form a *testudo*
behind a battering-ram.
One elbows
his way down the flue of the study,
where he finds the Grand Panjandrum

fast asleep
at the mahogany desk.
He blithely
clutches (1) a copy of *Thalaba*
and (2) the tortoise-shell powder-flask.

[*Putnam*]

§

Southey's lime-scaled pate with its scrofulous,
its scabrous diadem,

de dum,
lolls upon the other-worldly valise.

§

They strip him to the waist. The demagogue
is allowed one ladle of rum,

de dum,
from the keg

to help ward off the ram-
rods and switches and taws and tomahawks,

de dum, de dum,
wielded by the ghosts of a thousand Cayugas.

[*Chomsky*]

Several of whom begin to applaud.
He takes the plunge. Whereupon

he's in blood
stepp'd in so far . . . A furbelow of razor-ribbon

on which he'll come to grief.

[*Habermas*]

His head is swathed in a bloody turban.
The Cayugas remove the bolts

from their Accarbines
while the wet-set lay him on the pallet

and hook him up to the retinagraph.

[*Derrida*]

§

A glance back to the great palladium,
de dum,

as it goes up in flames.
Its voluminous

tulles and smoke-taffetas.
The fetid

stink of new-fangled creosote.
Tar-water. Tar-water and a sooty crust.

§

'At any moment now, the retina
will be in smithereens.'

§

The buckler affixed to the mast-head by a cleat
bears this device: a pair of gryphons

on a field of gold;
a scroll emblazoned with the word 'CROTONA'.

[*Harman*]

'Not "CROATAN", not "CROATOAN", but "CROTONA".'

[*Nozick*]

§

May, 1843. 'Catlin's Indian Gallery' has now reached Ireland. Half-way between Belfast and Dublin, near the present site of Unitel West, the medicine-bag is either misplaced or stolen.

§

May, 1846. President Polk engages a secret agent against Mexico. His name? 'Magoffin'.

§

May, 1873. The Modocs, led by Captain Jack, are systematically hunted down on the laver-breads of Oregon.

[*Kristeva*]

'Signifump. Signifump. Signifump.'

[*Hawking*]

§

The Cayugas have shouldered their Lasabers
and smoothed their scalp-locks.

A scrap of paper in a valise
now falls within the range

of a sensor-tile. The corridor
awash in slime. Trifoliate Chinese orange.

One leg held on by a frivolous
blood-garter.

§

It will all be over, de dum,
in next to no time –

long before 'The fluted cypresses
rear'd up their living obelisks'

has sent a shiver, de dum, de dum,
through Unitel, its iridescent Dome.

CPSIA information can be obtained
at www.ICGtesting.com
Printed in the USA
LVOW03s1947070218
565652LV00001B/9/P